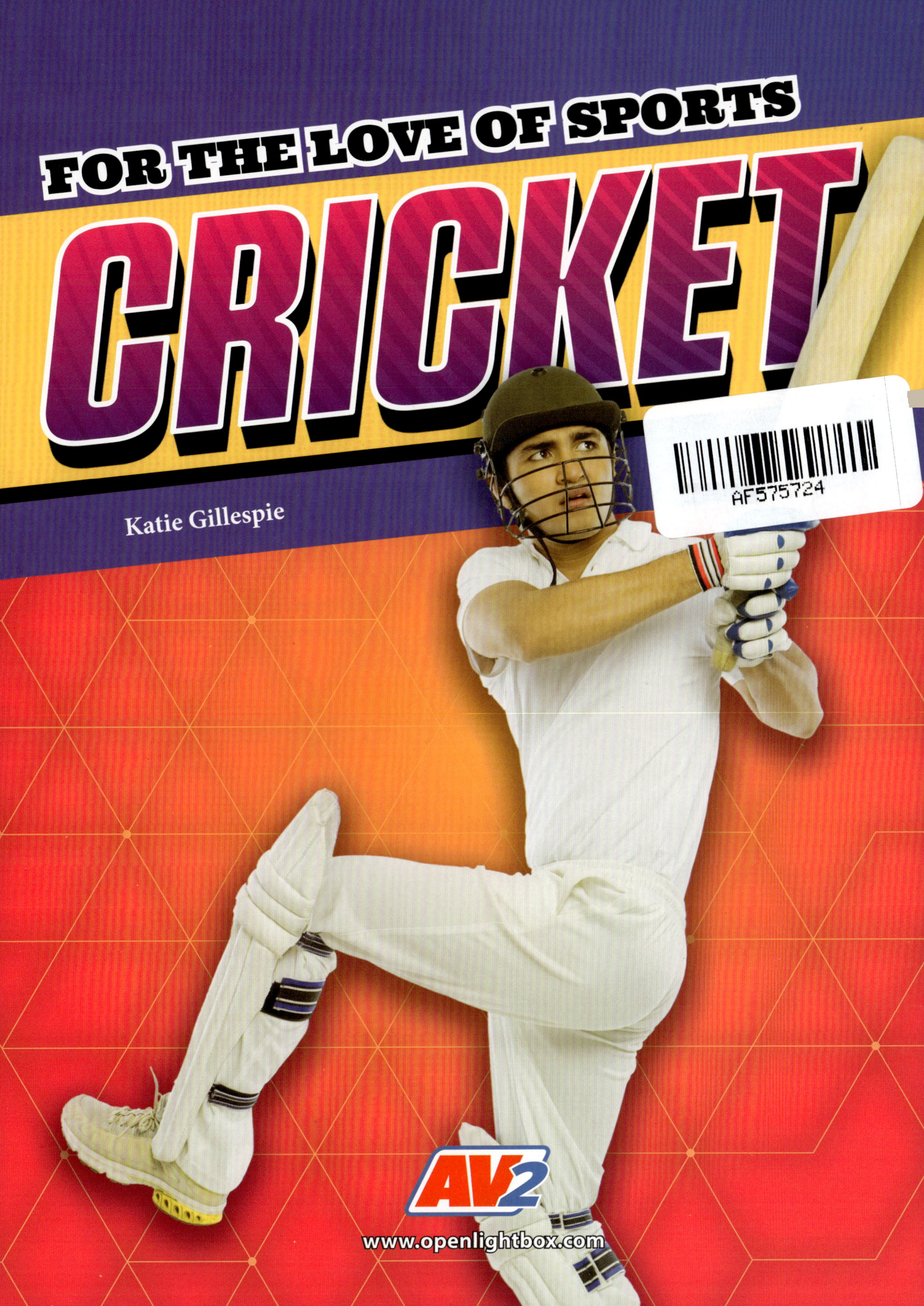

FOR THE LOVE OF SPORTS
CRICKET
Katie Gillespie
AF575724
AV2
www.openlightbox.com

Step 1
Go to **www.openlightbox.com**

Step 2
Enter this unique code
NQAYVBZKU

Step 3
Explore your interactive eBook!

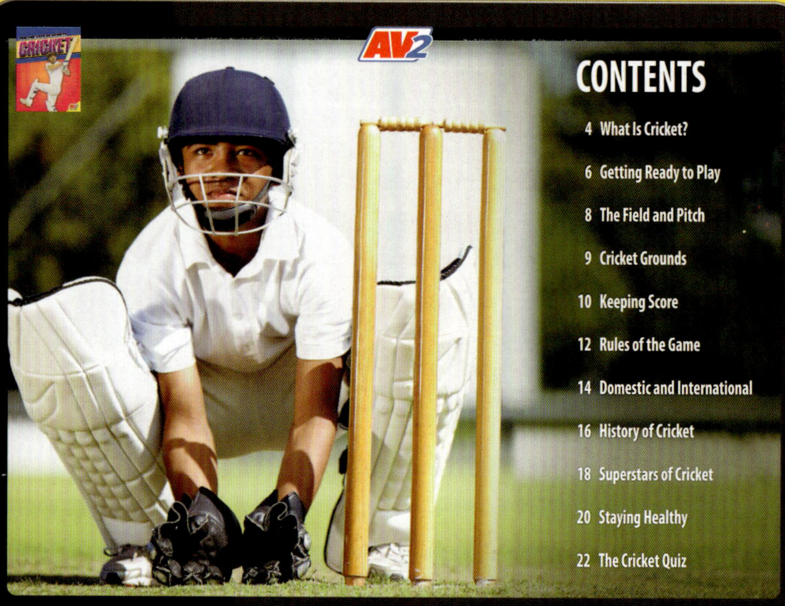

AV2 is optimized for use on any device

Your interactive eBook comes with...

Contents
Browse a live contents page to easily navigate through resources

Audio
Listen to sections of the book read aloud

Videos
Watch informative video clips

Weblinks
Gain additional information for research

Slideshows
View images and captions

Try This!
Complete activities and hands-on experiments

Key Words
Study vocabulary, and complete a matching word activity

Quizzes
Test your knowledge

Share
Share titles within your Learning Management System (LMS) or Library Circulation System

Citation
Create bibliographical references following APA, CMOS, and MLA styles

This title is part of our AV2 digital subscription

1-Year Grades K–5 Subscription
ISBN 978-1-7911-3320-7

Access hundreds of AV2 titles with our digital subscription.
Sign up for a FREE trial at **www.openlightbox.com/trial**

FOR THE LOVE OF SPORTS

CRICKET

CONTENTS

What Is Cricket?

Some experts believe that cricket was first played by children in England.

Cricket's origins are not known for certain, but may date back to 13th-century England. A more formal version of the sport, with organized **county** teams, developed in the 1600s. By the 1700s, cricket had become popular in London and other parts of England. Rules were written, and clubs were formed.

Cricket is played with a ball and a bat. In a cricket match, there are two opposing teams, each with 11 players. The teams take turns bowling and batting. Each turn is called an innings. The bowling team tries to hit a **wicket** with the ball. It is the bowling team's goal to get the batters dismissed, or "out." The batting team tries to hit the ball and score runs. Batters must keep the ball away from the wicket.

Modern cricket has three domestic formats and three international formats for matches. International matches are watched by fans all over the globe, especially in the United Kingdom, India, Pakistan, South Africa, New Zealand, and Australia. In fact, cricket is the second-most popular sport on the planet. Only soccer has more fans.

Cricket's name may have come from the Middle Dutch word *kricke*, which means "staff" or "stick."

Cricket has an estimated **2.5 billion fans** worldwide.

Virat Kohli is the only player to **average above 50 runs** in all three formats of international cricket.

The **"Timeless Test"** was the **longest** cricket match ever played, with **9 days of play**.

Getting Ready to Play

The two main pieces of equipment needed for cricket are the ball and the bat. The core of the ball is made of cork, which is a light, elastic material. It is covered in leather. Balls are traditionally red in color. However, white balls are also used, particularly for games taking place at night. Cricket bats are made of wood. They have a flat blade and a rounded handle. The handle is wrapped in rubber or leather for a better grip.

Cricket players often wear white clothing, or "cricket whites." This helps keep them cool in the hot sun. Players also need a variety of safety gear. Guards are made to protect different parts of the body. Some players may wear leg pads or gloves, too, depending on their position.

A cricket ball is hard and dense. In men's cricket, it must weigh between 5.5 and 5.75 ounces (156 and 163 grams).

Cricket bats come in many different sizes. The total length of a cricket bat should be 38 inches (96.5 centimeters) or less. This includes the handle. The blade cannot be broader than 4.25 inches (10.8 cm).

Wickets have three wooden stakes called stumps. The stumps are stuck into the ground at a height of 28 inches (71.1 cm).

Players often wear a cap to keep bright sunlight out of their eyes. Some players, usually batters and wicketkeepers, also wear helmets. These have a hard shell to protect the top of the head. A metal cage covers the jaw.

In the past, players almost always wore cricket whites. While these are still common, teams today may also dress in more colorful clothing. Shirts have short sleeves, and pants are loose and breathable.

Batters wear batting gloves that have dense foam padding around the fingers. The palms of the glove are thinner. Other players, such as wicketkeepers, may also wear gloves. These gloves are looser and less heavily padded than batting gloves.

Batters usually wear pads to cushion their knees and shins. Wicketkeepers have special pads that are smaller than batting pads. Players can also choose to wear arm, elbow, chest, abdomen, or thigh guards.

Cricket shoes vary in weight. Most have spikes on the bottom for traction. Players must choose shoes or boots that fit their position and playing style. The right footwear can also help protect players from ankle injuries.

The Field and Pitch

Cricket is played outdoors on a circular or oval-shaped field. The grass is level and mown close to the ground. The middle of the field has a rectangular area called the pitch. It measures 66 feet (20.12 meters) long and 10 feet (3.05 m) wide.

There are two wickets, each on opposite ends of the pitch. The three stumps of the wicket are placed close enough together that the ball cannot pass between them. The total width of the wicket is 9 inches (22.86 cm).

Two horizontal pieces of wood rest on top of each wicket. These are called the bails. They are 4.37 inches (11.1 cm) long. The bails must not extend past the stumps or rise more than 0.5 inches (1.27 cm) above them.

A boundary line marks the limits of the playing area. There are also lines on the pitch. They mark the **creases**. These include the batting crease, bowling crease, popping crease, and return creases.

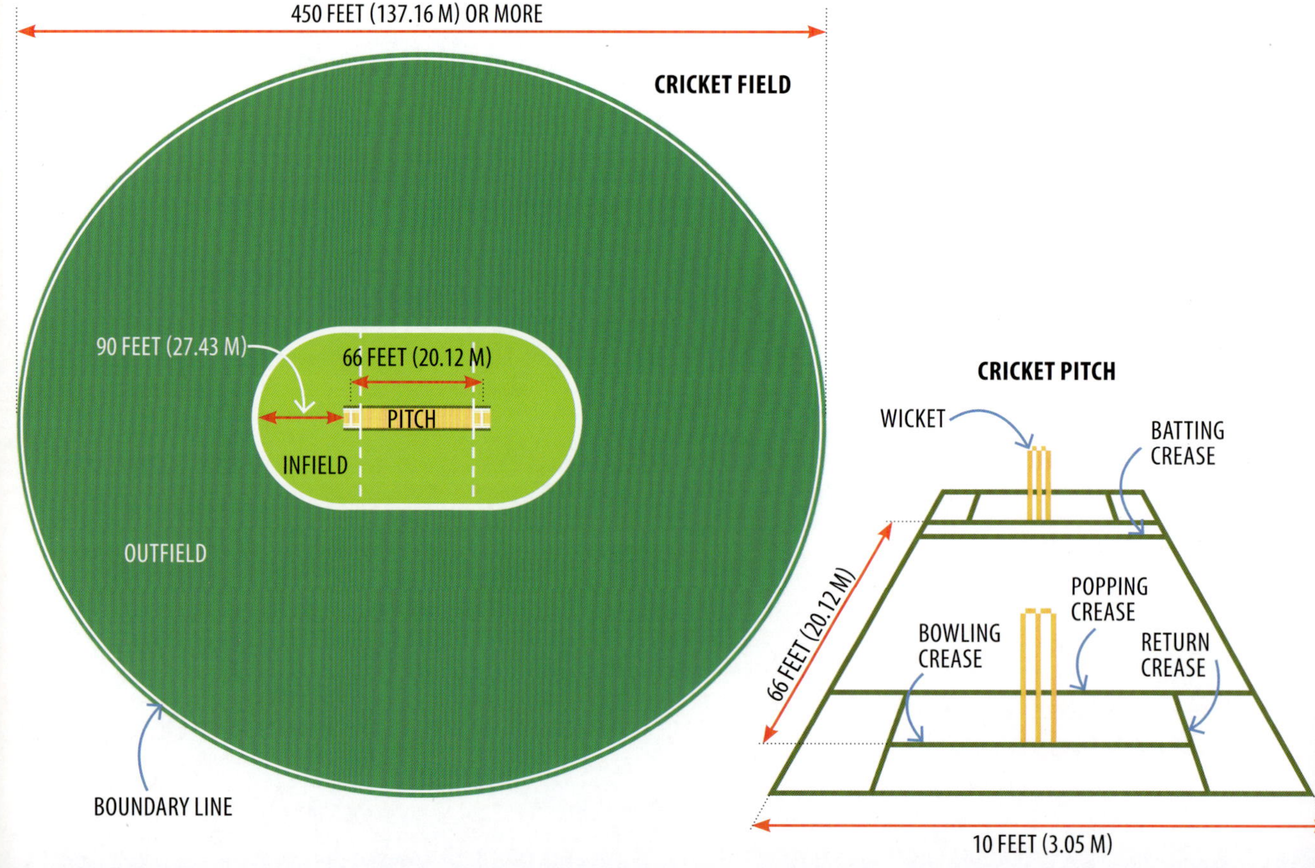

Cricket Grounds

Cricket is one of the world's most widely-watched **spectator** sports. Fans from across the globe cheer their teams to victory, and several iconic stadiums have been built to host cricket matches. Australia's Melbourne Cricket Ground is known for its size and beauty. Eden Gardens, in Kolkata, India, is often called the "Mecca of Indian Cricket." Lord's Cricket Ground and The Oval, both in the United Kingdom, are recognized for their rich history.

London, United Kingdom

Lord's Cricket Ground, in London, is likely the best-known cricket venue in the world. It is often called the "Home of Cricket." Lord's has hosted more Cricket World Cup finals than any other ground. Most recently, it hosted the 2019 Cricket World Cup finals between England and New Zealand.

Keeping Score

The main goal of cricket is to score as many runs as possible. Each team gets one or more chances to score runs. This happens during the team's turn to bat. The number of innings played depends on the format of the match. During an innings, one team bats. The other team bowls and fields. The team that ends with the most runs wins the match.

Cricket is typically a high-scoring sport. It is common for the final score to be in the hundreds.

There are only two members of the batting team on the field at a time. The batter who hits the ball is called the striker. The other batter is the nonstriker. As batters are dismissed from the game, new batters take their place on the pitch. All 11 members of the bowling team are on the field at once. One of these players acts as the bowler. Another is the wicketkeeper. The other nine members of this team are fielders. Once an innings is done, the teams switch places.

A batter has two objectives. First, he or she must protect the wicket to avoid being dismissed. The batter does this by making defensive hits. This kind of hit keeps the ball away from the wicket. However, there may not be enough time to run after a defensive hit. In this case, the batter simply waits for another ball to be bowled.

Second, batters need to score runs. There are a few different ways in which runs can be scored. When the striker hits the ball away, the batters can switch places, each running to the other side of the pitch. If they are both able to make it to the opposite wicket, one run is scored. They can continue running back and forth multiple times, as long as they are not dismissed by the fielding team. Each time they make it successfully from one side of the pitch to the other, an additional run is scored. Runs can also be scored by hitting the ball to the boundary. If the ball hits the ground and reaches the boundary, four runs are scored. A ball that makes it over the line without hitting the ground is worth six runs.

Team captains toss a coin at the start of a match. The winner decides which team will bat first and which team will bowl.

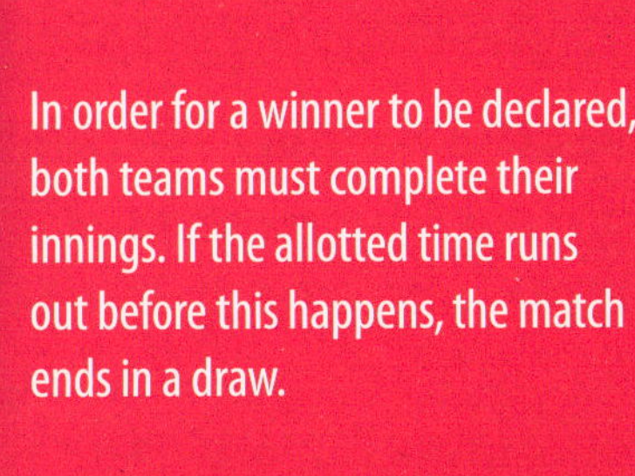

In order for a winner to be declared, both teams must complete their innings. If the allotted time runs out before this happens, the match ends in a draw.

Rules of the Game

The bowling team has two main objectives. One is to try to dismiss the batters from the other team. The other is to prevent runs from being scored. To accomplish this, the bowler, wicketkeeper, and fielders all play a role.

It is the bowler's job to pitch the ball to the opposing team's striker, with the aim of hitting the wicket with the ball. A bowler can only pitch six balls in a row, each to the same wicket. This is called an over. Once an over is completed, a new bowler from the same team takes over the role. This bowler targets the opposite wicket.

The wicketkeeper crouches behind the striker's wicket. He or she tries to catch the ball if the striker does not hit it away. If the ball is hit, the fielders must chase after it.

There are a number of different ways in which a batter can be dismissed. Some are common, while others are uncommon. Many of the most common ways involve the wicket.

Bowlers can run for as many steps as they like before pitching, as long as they do not cross the popping crease.

If one or both bails fall off the stumps of the wicket, or a stump is knocked out of the ground, the wicket is said to be put down, and the batter is dismissed. This is fairly common and happens when the bowler pitches the ball into the stumps. It can also happen if the batter accidentally hits the wicket.

If a member of the bowling team is able to put down the wicket with the ball while the batter is running outside of the crease, the batter is also dismissed. The **umpire** may judge the batter out by the leg before wicket (LBW) rule as well. This means that the bowler's pitch would have hit the stumps had the batter's leg or pads not been in the way. Another common way for a batter to be dismissed is if he or she hits a ball away and a fielder catches it before it touches the ground.

A male batter is usually referred to as a batsman.

Fielders often adjust their positions depending on whether the batter is right- or left-handed.

Domestic and International

The three basic forms of domestic cricket are First Class, One Day (OD), and Twenty20 (T20). There are some key differences between each form. These include the amount of overs bowled, the length of the match, and the number of innings played.

First Class cricket has unlimited overs. This means there is no maximum limit to the total number of overs bowled. An innings ends when 10 of the 11 batters are dismissed. Teams usually bat two innings each, and matches take about three to five days. Play lasts for six hours per day.

When cricket first began, there were only two different types of matches. These were First Class and Test.

During Test matches, players wear traditional cricket whites and use a red ball. In ODI and T20I, the uniforms are much more colorful, and the ball is white.

OD and T20 both have limited overs. In OD matches, there are usually 50 overs per innings. Play takes place over a single day. T20 cricket is even shorter. Matches have 20 overs per innings and last about three hours. In OD and T20, teams bat one innings each. If 10 of the 11 batters are dismissed before all the overs are bowled, the innings still ends.

At the international level, the three formats are known as Test, One Day International (ODI), and Twenty 20 International (T20I). Test matches are a form of First Class cricket.

International matches are overseen by the International Cricket Council (ICC). This global organization works to govern the sport of cricket. It is responsible for the playing conditions, code of conduct, and other regulations that govern international games.

The ICC runs several major tournaments, such as the ICC World Test Championship for Test cricket, the ICC Cricket World Cup for ODI cricket, and the ICC T20 World Cup for T20I cricket. It also provides the officials that preside over matches.

T20 was introduced in 2003. This faster, more action-packed version of cricket brought a whole new audience to the sport.

The ICC was formed in 1909 by representatives from Australia, England, and South Africa. Today, it has more than 100 member countries.

History of Cricket

Since its early beginnings in England, cricket's popularity has only grown. It is now a favorite around the world. Over the years, countless milestones have been achieved in this sport.

The first Test match took place in 1877. Played between Australia and England, it started an enduring rivalry. Today, Test matches played between these two countries are considered part of a series called the Ashes.

1744 The first set of cricket rules are written. They are printed on a silk handkerchief.

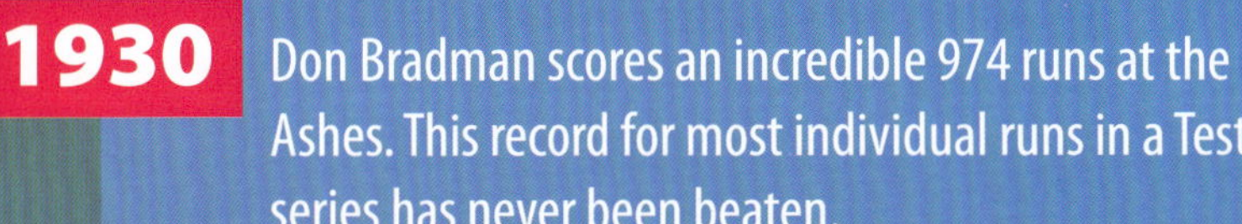

1930 Don Bradman scores an incredible 974 runs at the Ashes. This record for most individual runs in a Test series has never been beaten.

1958 The International Women's Cricket Council (IWCC) is formed. Its founding members are Australia, England, South Africa, New Zealand, and the Netherlands.

1975 The first Cricket World Cup is held in England. West Indies wins the finals, beating Australia by 17 runs.

2003 India's Shoaib Akhtar bowls the fastest delivery in cricket history, pitching the ball at a speed of 100.2 miles (161.3 kilometers) per hour.

2021 Australia defeats New Zealand at the ICC Men's T20 World Cup. This is the country's first T20 World Cup win.

The shortest Test match had only ***50 minutes of play****. It was held in 1926.*

Women's cricket *has been overseen by the* ***ICC*** *since* ***2005****, when the ICC and the IWCC merged.*

In ***2018, Mithali Raj*** *became the first Indian cricketer to* ***score 2,000 runs in T20Is****.*

Superstars of Cricket

There have been many outstanding cricketers from around the world. Their achievements inspire today's athletes.

Sir Donald Bradman

BIRTH DATE: August 27, 1908
HOMETOWN: Cootamundra, Australia

CAREER FACTS:

- Bradman is remembered as the greatest cricket player of the 20th century.
- He set the record for most runs scored in a day in a Test match, with 309. This record still stands today.
- Bradman also holds the record for the highest career batting average. His average of 99.94 is 38.07 ahead of the closest runner-up.
- He was **knighted** in 1949, the same year he retired from First Class cricket.
- Over his career, Bradman scored a total of 6,996 Test runs and 28,067 First Class runs.

Sachin Tendulkar

BIRTH DATE: April 24, 1973
HOMETOWN: Mumbai, India

CAREER FACTS:

- Tendulkar is widely considered the greatest batsman of the modern era. He is known as the "God of Cricket" and the "Master Blaster."
- He made his Test cricket debut in 1989, at age 16.
- In 2012, he became the first person to ever score 100 international **centuries**.
- Tendulkar holds the records for the most career runs in both ODI and Test matches. He scored 18,426 ODI runs and 15,921 Test runs.
- In 2019, Tendulkar was inducted into the ICC Hall of Fame.

MS Dhoni

BIRTH DATE: July 7, 1981
HOMETOWN: Ranchi, India

CAREER FACTS:

- Dhoni was successful as both a wicketkeeper and a batsman, and has been called the best **finisher** in cricket history.
- As the captain, or "skipper," of India's national cricket team, he led India to more Test wins than any other captain, with 27.
- Dhoni received the ICC ODI Player of the Year Award two years in a row, in 2008 and 2009.
- His performance in the 2011 ODI World Cup helped India win the final.

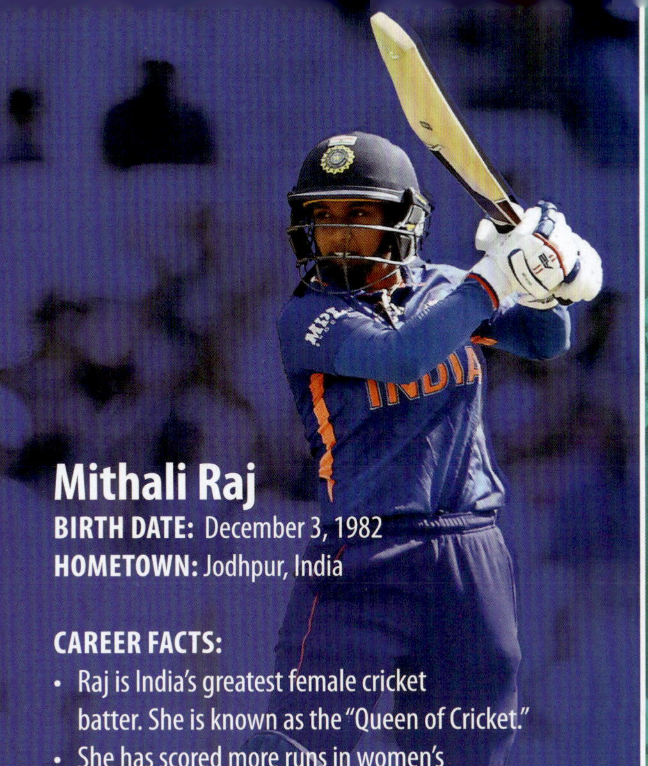

Mithali Raj

BIRTH DATE: December 3, 1982
HOMETOWN: Jodhpur, India

CAREER FACTS:

- Raj is India's greatest female cricket batter. She is known as the "Queen of Cricket."
- She has scored more runs in women's international cricket than any other player.
- At her ODI debut, Raj scored an **unbeaten** 114 runs. She was only 16 at the time.
- In 2002, Raj achieved her highest Test score, with 214 runs. This broke a world record.
- She captained the Indian women's national team to its first World Cup final in 2005.

Virat Kohli

BIRTH DATE: November 5, 1988
HOMETOWN: Delhi, India

CAREER FACTS:

- Kohli's nickname is "King Kohli." He is one of the best batsmen ever to play the game.
- He became the captain of Team India after MS Dhoni stepped down.
- Kohli holds the record for the most T20I player-of-the-series awards, with 7.
- He has the highest T20I career batting average in the world.
- Kohli reached 10,000 ODI runs faster than any other batsman in the world. He did it in 205 innings, breaking the previous record held by Sachin Tendulkar.

Sarah Jane Taylor

BIRTH DATE: May 20, 1989
HOMETOWN: London, United Kingdom

CAREER FACTS:

- Taylor is one of the best wicketkeepers of all time.
- She was named the ICC Women's T20I Cricketer of the Year in 2013.
- Taylor is a double World Cup champion. Her team won in both 2009 and 2017.
- She has 100 career **stumpings** in international cricket, more than any other female cricketer.

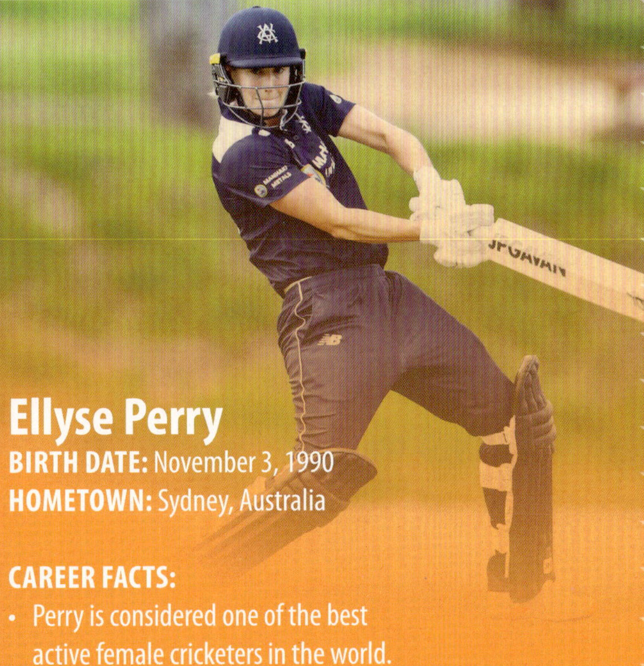

Ellyse Perry

BIRTH DATE: November 3, 1990
HOMETOWN: Sydney, Australia

CAREER FACTS:

- Perry is considered one of the best active female cricketers in the world.
- In addition to cricket, she has also played professional soccer.
- Perry has appeared in World Cups for both cricket and soccer. She was the first Australian to do so.
- Perry made history as the youngest Australian ever to play international cricket. She made her debut at age 16.
- She is the first T20I player with 1,000 runs and 100 wickets.

Staying Healthy

Cricket players need different kinds of meals at particular times. What they eat and when depends on the physical activity they will be doing. There are three main categories of meals. These are pre-game, training or competition, and recovery.

Before a game, players must fuel up their bodies. They also need to make sure they are well **hydrated**. Cricketers should eat a large meal two to four hours before playing. After a game, they should eat a recovery meal. Protein, found in foods such as eggs, meat, and nuts, repairs muscle. Carbohydrates aid in refueling the body. They can be found in oats and sweet potatoes.

Drinking ice water or sports drinks allows athletes to stay cool and hydrated in hot weather.

Vegetables such as broccoli, spinach, and carrots have nutrients that can help revitalize a player after a big match.

Cricket players need good batting and bowling techniques. They can develop these essential skills through practice. For example, legendary batsman Don Bradman used to do a simple drill with a golf ball. He would hit it repeatedly against a water tank. The unpredictable rebounds helped him learn hand-eye coordination.

Whether bowling, batting, or fielding, cricket players all rely on their shoulders. This puts them at high risk for **rotator cuff** damage, one of the most common injuries in cricket. If any of the muscles in the rotator cuff are torn or strained, it can be very painful to play. Doing strengthening exercises can be helpful.

Ankle and hamstring sprains may happen when running or quickly changing directions. Warming up before playing cricket helps reduce the risk of these kinds of injuries.

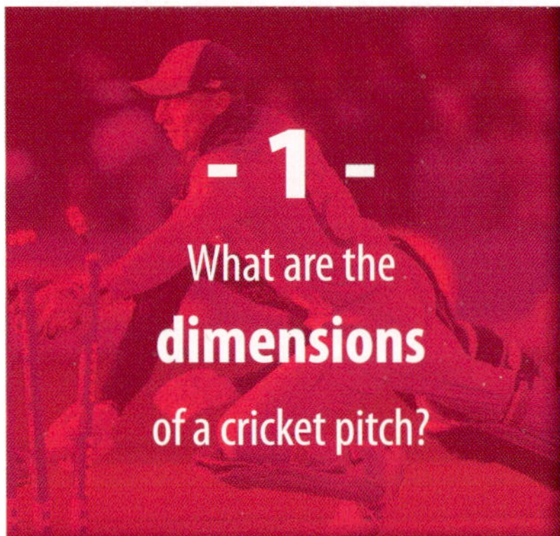

- 1 -

What are the **dimensions** of a cricket pitch?

- 2 -

When was the **first cricket World Cup** held?

- 3 -

What is one of the most **common injuries** in cricket?

THE CRICKET QUIZ

- 4 -

How **many players** are on a cricket **team**?

- 5 -

What are the **three formats** of international cricket?

- 6 -

What is the **main goal** of cricket?

- 7 -

Who is known as the **"God of Cricket"**?

- 8 -

What **color** is a **traditional cricket ball**?

- 9 -

How **many** ways are there to get a **batter dismissed**?

- 10 -

Where is **Lord's Cricket Ground**?

ANSWERS: 1 66 feet (20.12 m) long by 10 feet (3.05 m) wide 2 In 1975 3 Rotator cuff damage 4 11 5 Test, ODI, and T20I 6 To score as many runs as possible 7 Sachin Tendulkar 8 Red 9 10 10 London, United Kingdom

Key Words

centuries: 100 runs in a single innings

county: a specific region of a state or country

creases: lines that form a box around the wickets, marking where players must stand

finisher: in limited overs cricket, a batter who is able to finish an innings during a high-pressure situation

hydrated: provided with water to maintain a proper balance of fluids

knighted: given the title of "knight" by a British monarch, usually for outstanding achievements

rotator cuff: a group of four muscles found at the shoulder

spectator: someone who watches an event, but does not participate

stumpings: when the wicketkeeper knocks the bails off the stumps before the batter gets behind the batting crease

umpire: the person who makes sure the rules are followed during a match

unbeaten: finished the game without being dismissed

wicket: a set of three stumps with two bails on top

Index

Get the best of both worlds.

AV2 bridges the gap between print and digital.

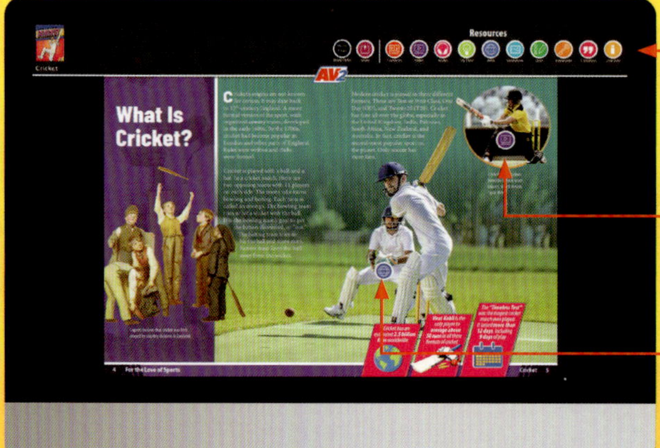

The expandable resources toolbar enables quick access to content including **videos**, **audio**, **activities**, **weblinks**, **slideshows**, **quizzes**, and **key words**.

Animated videos make static images come alive.

Resource icons on each page help readers to further **explore key concepts**.

Published by Lightbox Learning Inc.
276 5th Avenue, Suite 704 #917
New York, NY 10001
Website: www.openlightbox.com

Library of Congress Cataloging-in-Publication Data

Names: Gillespie, Katie, author.
Title: Cricket / Katie Gillespie.
Description: New York : Lightbox Learning Inc., 2023. | Series: For the love of sports | Includes index. | Audience: Grades 4-6
Identifiers: LCCN 2022011687 (print) | LCCN 2022011688 (ebook) | ISBN 9781791146108 (library binding) | ISBN 9781791146115 (paperback) | ISBN 9781791146122
Subjects: LCSH: Cricket--Juvenile literature.
Classification: LCC GV917 .G55 2023 (print) | LCC GV917 (ebook) | DDC 796.358--dc23/eng/20220509
LC record available at https://lccn.loc.gov/2022011687
LC ebook record available at https://lccn.loc.gov/2022011688

Printed in Guangzhou, China
1 2 3 4 5 6 7 8 9 0 26 25 24 23 22

122022
101121

Project Coordinator Priyanka Das
Art Director Terry Paulhus
Layout Jean Faye Marie Rodriguez

Photo Credits
Every reasonable effort has been made to trace ownership and to obtain permission to reprint copyright material. The publisher would be pleased to have any errors or omissions brought to its attention so that they may be corrected in subsequent printings. The publisher acknowledges Alamy, Bridgeman Images, Dreamstime, Getty Images, and Shutterstock as its primary image suppliers for this title.